GW00858501

CREATOR

CREATOR

ROBERT D. MACKAY

XULON PRESS

Xulon Press
2301 Lucien Way #415
Maitland, FL 32751
407.339.4217
www.xulonpress.com

Printed in the United States of America.

ISBN-13: 978-1-6305-0652-0

TABLE OF CONTENTS

Creator

INTRODUCTION

I was saved in June of 2000. My walk with the Lord began with a simple cry for help. I was a drunk drowning in my addiction. I was desperate and asked God, a God I did not believe in, to please help me, and He did. I have not had a drink or even had a desire to drink from that day to this. Two weeks later, I gave my heart to Christ, and I haven't looked back. My journey of faith has not always been easy but it has been amazing in so many ways.

My first real test of faith came about five months into my walk with God, one morning as I was reading the creation account in the book of Genesis. I remember the feeling of wonder I had, imagining the earth in its early stages being shaped by the word of God. It was amazing until I realized deep down inside that I didn't believe it. You see, I was raised in a culture that taught evolution as the source of all life. I was a sold-out believer in the theory of randomly formed life. I was stunned because if the first words in the Bible were not true, then what else should I be questioning? I asked God for an answer and put down my Bible, vowing not to read another word until I heard from the Lord.

The very next morning I got up early, before sunrise, and sat on my porch with my cup of coffee and waited for God to show me the way past this unbelief in my heart. I knew God would answer because I was sober, and that was my first miracle and one I could clearly recognize as a miracle. Anyone reading this who has ever wrestled with addiction will know what I am talking about. As the first rays of sunlight began to make themselves known, a little bird flew onto my porch. He was looking for sugar in a small feeder I had hanging in the corner. He was a common bird; we call them sugar birds, though the real name for them is a banana quit. As I watched this simple little bird flying from the feeder to the arm of a chair next to me, I felt the presence of God. He opened my eyes and allowed me to see this simple creature in a way I had never seen it before. I remember being fascinated with the way it moved. I could see it look at me with an intelligence I could almost feel. The feathers on its wings, the way the tiny feet gripped the feeder... all of it leapt out at me and captured my attention. In that moment, I heard a still small voice say, "Does that look like an accident?" I remember saying softly, "Of course not," and the voice answered, "Can we move on now."

What the enemy tried to use to shake my faith is now one of the strongest pieces of evidence I have to support my faith. If we simply stop and look around us for a moment, we can see the evidence of God in every detail. *Creator* was written to share that revelation. I hope these poems touch your heart.

Blessings
Robert Mackay

ACKNOWLEDGEMENTS

B efore diving in I would like to take a moment to thank some special people who helped make this book possible. To Kellie Cory, thank you for reading the poems as I wrote them and adding your artistic touch to the ones that spoke loudest to you. I appreciate your insight and special touch. You added to the vision and I thank you for your joyful energy and support.

To Troy Sextius, thank you for painting the perfect cover art long before the first words of the book were written. From the first moment I saw your painting it spoke to me. You painted a spiritual marker for me to see and remember that God is good!

Most all thank you Jesus! You answered the prayer of a desperate man and delivered me from my own mess. You have blessed me with a beautiful wife and family and made every day a second chance at having the life I was made for before the beginning of time. Thank you for your sacrifice and ever-lasting love!

CREATOR'S WILL

What is nothing?
A term unknown and unfounded,
For there was always Creator.

Before time began, He spoke the first stroke of the hand
That made everything.

Light...a gift for eyes yet unmade,
Earth for mud and dust,
Colors for flowers, blue for oceans,
Black for angry sky...who shall question why?

Man shall question why.
Am I God's own image?

...Or God Himself?
For we love to rule our fleeting lives,
While the ones who made us watch and know all we do not.

For blindness is a spiritual disease
Commonly inflicted on those of us who will not be ruled

Even by love Itself.

WHAT WAS MADE

Did the first lion roar or merely purr as God ruf-
fled his mane?
I think he purred and rolled around the feet of the one who
loved him.
To be that cat, unafraid, without awe, only knowing the joy

Of God's loving touch.

Did zebra jump and prance with every finger-stroked stripe?
Did monkey chatter from the trees as man rose from
bended knees

To look God in the eye?

What of the flowers
Freshly painted in my Lord's mind everyday?
So perfect, they weep glory
And sing a story of perfected love.

No lust, no anger, no longing or strife,
Only life
beneath trees tended in the very presence of God.

Meals freshly picked, bursting with juice
Dripping from laughing chins, no fetters to hold off sins,
For love was truly free in Eden time,

Truly free for all to be His.

ROCK

Picked from the heart of many
I have turned it time and again and wondered,
Is it a weapon?
Something formed to kill those that offend me?
Or is it a piece of slag from the forge
That made the mountains and the valleys?

Is it merely cosmic dust joined by heat, a bang so big
It explains everything?

Or is it a whittling of the Master?
A tiny piece carefully shaved away from the perfection.

Is it future fodder for the making of men,
Raised up for such a time as this?

Does it cry out at the thought of God
In a tone too low for me to hear?

Or is it evidence of a crime,
Testimony against those who would say,
"From nothing evolves something"?

Maybe it is really just a gift,
Something I may skip across the water
And wonder at the rippling wake it makes.

LONG DENIED

God is dead,
Or so he said as he drove one more seed deep into the earth,
Freshly turned, smelling sweetly of life to come.

I shook my head doubting as I looked at the seed
Lying in my hand.
But he seemed so sure that I did not think he could be wrong.

"Hard work is key; make with your own hands.
Nothing is free; take it from me.
No one cares about you; someday you'll see."

It seemed a daunting thing, there in the withering sun,
Burying seeds one by one,
To know my fate lay in my own bleeding hands.

Days later, as we gazed over that burning ground,
Dry and parched,
My granddaddy cursed heaven for the lack of rain.

As for me,

I chose to close my eyes tight and dream of thunder,
Thanking my God for patience
And the beautiful gift of rainbows.

GRANDMA'S TABLE

The dark wood makes me sneeze as I sand it,
Working with the grain,
Watching it lighten beneath the onslaught of grit and sweat,
The sap wood borders, the tight grain, marking the
years of life

Before the harvest.

Each tracing line is unique in width and followed curve.
I remember the crystal candy jar that rested here as a child,
The source of endless chocolate treats and cello-
phane-wrapped butterscotch.
I can see the beautiful top hidden by torn wrapping paper
every Christmas.
There is life in every scratch and mark I slowly sand away
Till she is ready for the gift of new life.

A fresh anointing of tung oil rubbed to a glossy shine,
Ready for my children's memories to be etched by daily use,
Baptized in spilled juice and marker stains.

A rich legacy for a fallen tree
That started life as a seed smaller than a dime.

BIRD SONG

Little bird, come talk to me of God.
Dance from limb to limb
And speak of truth plainly seen
In the sheen of delicate feathers that flit you from
place to place,
Sipping from flowers,
Bathing in showers from the garden fountain.
Little bird, sing bigger words
Than all modern science can refute.
Exist this day so all may know
God sends His breath
And it is how we are filled with wonder.

SAILOR'S REWARD

The coffee settled to my belly in a lava trail
So hot but needed.
The night was longer than most,
A full night blinded and beating into the wind.
The seas worked against us in the ocean's relentless way,
But the reward was near.
My little lady pitched and fought the reign
Like a thoroughbred released from the stable then forced to
walk not run.
Every stay hummed and sail fluttered, balanced on the
edge of luff.
All night she had pulled for her head
The chance to run in the wind,
But soon she would have it,
A close reach for Road Town,
Racing in the trough like a made pair set for freedom's gate—
A cherry red eastern sky,
Hot black coffee passing salty lips,
Such sweet promise in this new day.

EVIDENCE

I can close my eyes and smell the scent of the sea lapping
at my feet.

I have seen the hand of God whip the ocean to fury,
Only to calm it and paint the surface in mirrored tranquility.
I have seen corals teeming with creatures so bright,
They shame the flowers bowing down the trees.

I have seen marlin burst through the realm of sea to sky
And dance upon the waves in twisting rage.
I have seen whales blow contempt at the weighted ones stuck
upon the shore
Then dive deep and be seen no more.

I have seen frigate birds frolicking on the morning drafts,
Launched to the heavens by invisible hands,
Gone to chase the fish that fly above the waves
Trying to escape certain death in the dolphin's grasp.

I have seen all these things and know
God is great as I feel His sandy grit tickling my toes.

TABU

She was a jumper in her youth,
A runner of infinite grace,
Eager to please and quick to learn
With a quiet peace in her eyes as they followed my
every move.

So faithful, so loyal, and without reproach,
A favorite in her master's eye,
She often must have wondered at my leaving
For a family not her own.

For her love was one that did not tolerate others
Being too close to the one to whom she was devoted,
And so she lived apart until the time of reckoning,
When our relationship ended in sleep
Deep and unyielding.

Sleep, my love, and rest in my heart and mind
As I scratched those ears a final time
And whispered, "Good girl," as the light left those gentle eyes
Forever...

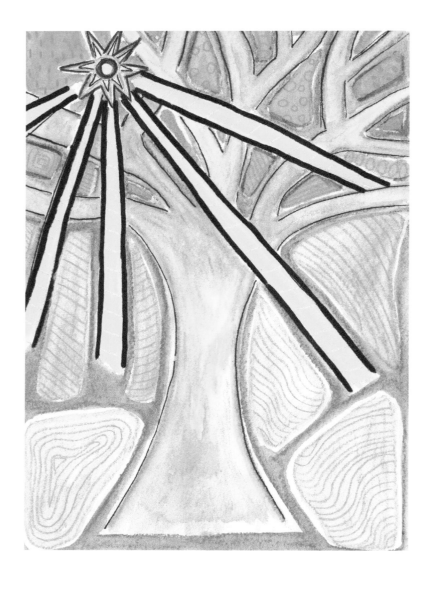

THE TEST OF THE TREE

She was a good tree,
Perfect for climbing and learning limits
Or new challenges for the stronger hearts.

I can still taste the sweet fruit gathered in leafy shade,
Lounging in a comfortable cleft, my favorite part,
As I watched my crazy cousin tempt fate
One more time.

For some are unfazed by simple laws like gravity
And the promise of pain at the proving
Even careful climbing was no guarantee of safety,
As I proved more times than not.

But the need to prove my manly traits
Often moved me toward dangerous feats,
Remembering the joy of success,
Forgetting the agony of failure.

Survival was a gift from God,
The memories a reminder of Grace
Given even before obedience was lain
At the feet of my Savior.

For now I know what is hard is not impossible
And what seems impossible
Is easy in the Will of God.

WHAT IS POSSIBLE?

"Mary must have known a man to have a son.
It's plain to see; Jesus can't have been born immaculately."
As a doctor and an educated man, he spoke with authority,
A modern day Pharisee for the atheistic tribe.

I smiled and held my pearls tightly.
With a deep breath, I glanced up at the stars in the sky,
Gathering my spiritual evidence, putting down my perceived right
To be angry at the slander of my Savior's heritage.

For the night air still held the scent of fresh rain,
Gracefully given by a loving God,
And the sun promised to rise tomorrow and bring its light
To this darkened place; so, with a smile on my face,

I said, "God knows."

DESTINED

The rigging strains to hold the breeze, laying the rails awash,
And the course is set to a purpose somewhere ahead,
An unmarked highway that leads to adventure
As duty drifts further astern.

The frigate bird shadows high, picking flying fish
from the waves
As they desperately dash from the predatory push of the bow,
For the raw reality is eat and be eaten here above the
ocean floor
That lays a thousand fathoms beneath this flimsy vessel's keel.

Here, far from my native land, I glide by the grace of God,
Learning to understand how little I know
Of all there is around me and below.
My ignorance is a breathtaking fact of life.

It points me to a trust that no amount of knowledge
can provide,
The reality that I must release the outcome of my fate
To the one who made all I see here with my naked
human eyes
And rest in this gift of peace

That surpasses all understanding.

CHURCH OF THE HIGH COUNTRY

I have walked days from the end of the last road,
Camping alone beneath a shrinking sliver of a moon,

Seeking in the Church of the High Country.

I walked beside a crystal lake today, mirroring heaven's
perfection,
Stopping now and again to listen to the roar of dragonflies,

Sanctuary in the Church of the High Country.

Staring at my fire, wondering at the delicate dance of
the embers,
Feeling my excitement rise at the sight of fireflies
Glinting in the evening breeze,

Worshiping in the Church of the High Country.

Here at the end of my final day, in sweet meadow grass I lay,
Waiting for a moonless black curtain to fall
Here, where I can see it all.

As light fades, the Glory rises;
Sweeping stars march across the void of nothing,
And my tiny eyes are filled to bursting,

Communion in the Church of the High Country.

Northern Lights

Island boys seldom see miracles such as these.
Stars are a common thing close to the equator;
Those I have tried counting many times and failed.

But here on deck, watching the heavens dance,
I am lost again in God's immensity,
Staring at these lights He placed in the sky for me.

I am held captive by the wonder
Of light charging into the curtain of night,
Leaving a fleeting trace of bright renewed.

God's subtle neon cry of love
Splashed upon this northern sky
High above the ink-drenched sea.

SEA

Rustling fronds dance in the breeze
As the sea sings up and down the shore;
Waves cry for grace beneath a rainbow
So close but away.

This is a day the Lord made,
Brutal heat beside the cooling sea,
Relief and reminder so close
They cannot drift far from mind.

As I look out at the mirror
Glistening back upon my eye,
Cooling sea, bluer sky
As the life we live

Slides by...

LIFE

What is my life?
A pumping heart, a flood of blood,
Swelling veins...

Is it pain and pleasure forced to meet
In this broken vessel?
Is it even me, small and insignificant?

Am I fearfully and wonderfully made

As He says,

Or mad to believe anyone cares?

What is my life
Other than a miracle,
More than any random meeting of egg and sperm?

I Am has said I am His,
And in this I rejoice as my heart pumps
And blood flows
To an ever higher purpose.

I will face the dawn with joy
Red in the morning; devil take warning,
For light has come,
And by God's grace I am free.

Take Measure and Know

Man of science, tell me the full measure of the sky,
From its start in the east
To the tail of the west; how great a sky is it?
How many years of light must we wait for an answer,
And what great number will we hear?

Or maybe how high a sky is the better question,
Stratosphere, far out of here, high.
The first star is barely off the ground when we compare
Here to there, somewhere beyond our knowing.

The sun is warm, this we know, melting snow in the spring,
Yet colder nights bring smaller lights in infinite number.
Shall we count them all for the next hundred years,
or simply smile and wonder with our hearts full of truth?

QUIET PLACE

I lay here seeking beneath the trees,
Swinging slowly in the cooling breeze.
So sweet the shade on a summer's day;
Lying here silent, I gently sway.
The leaves, they rustle a simple song
As the birds chant the chorus pure and strong.
I close my eyes and dream of grace
Here in the castle of my quiet place.
My God, come meet me; hold my hand.
Soften my heart as only You can.
Replace my fear with unrivaled love.
Drive out my anger; send forth the dove.
May Your Spirit touch my wounded soul.
Bring forth healing, the purging coal.
Help me to leave my dead man behind,
For now that I see, let me no longer be blind.
For Your truth, it surrounds me under these trees.
Your voice calls me out saying You are well pleased
To call me Your son bought by blood and by grace
As we meet here and counsel in the quiet place.
For this is the thing that I most need to do:
Stop in this moment and just talk to You,
So I know Your will and plan for my day.
Lord, thank you for meeting me here as I pray.

EARTH

Lay my body here in the ground.
In a simple pine coffin, let it go down
Next to the roots of the old mango tree,
The giver of fruit sweet as can be.

For God took from the earth and brought forth man,
Adam and Eve, in His perfect plan.
Abraham, Moses, Jesus, and you
Are made by a God who can make Angels from dew.

Stones will cry out, mountains will fall
Just to give praise to the God of us all,
So lay me down here in this simple pine box,
Here in the earth made from mountains and rocks.

For my soul is with God, high by His throne,
Bought with a price and called as His own.
A brother to God who hung on a tree,
That's who I am, and that's who I'll be.

So as you eat mangos here in the shade,
Bending the grass that grows root to blade,
I'll be with Jesus as eternities pass
In a peace that has been here from the first to the last.

DEEP OCEAN

Deep ocean hums praise,
A sweet swelling beat few seek to hear,
Way out here, far from land.

No birds cry or flowers bloom,
Yet God's voice rushes with the cresting sea,
Calling me gently.

I trim the main to gain inches
Toward a place which seems an eternity away,
Day after day.

But now a peace reigns eternal,
Lest God bring forth the rage to trouble the fearless
Humbled by helplessness.

For so gentle a home to turn
Is sometimes the will of my master, our God,
A humility taught.

For the humble heart hears this subtle rhythm,
Deep ocean swaying to the beat of life,
Singing gently,

All praise to God.

HEAVY HORSE

He was a monstrous breed,
All shire, with hooves the size of dinner plates.
He tossed his head once, and I cleared the ground,
Hanging from the lead like a gutted fish.
But he set me down and stole my hat
In way of apology.

His job was to remind us of a simpler time
Before oil and diesel ruled the harvest and the toil,
When heavy horse leaned into leather and so turned the soil.
For Goliath knew the feel of tack, and he could pull,
As his great grandsire did in times of war
And his mother too and hers before.

Back to the time of King Arthur and Sir Gallahad,
When Scottish stone was turned into endless mile of wall,
And heavy wagons hauled it all, here to there,
Coal and stone, combines and sleds moved by the might
of beasts,
Gentle giants of progress forgotten in the wake of
greater things
Now standing quietly under the indignity of ribbons in a
braided mane.

THE CANDY TREE

Have you truly tasted fruit?
Not merely sweet but decadent sweet,

Strawberries ripe and ruby red,
Blueberries plump and swelled to bursting,

Raspberries ripened on the path to somewhere,
Sweet snack placed for pleasure,
Sweet snack meant as treasure to the tongue.

Have you held a Mango so ripe with promised taste?
The skin scent of it waters the mouth with anticipation,
A pleasure path remembered and wandered many
times before.

For God so loves us all, He places presents in the trees,
Created taste buds that would please,
And hid His candies in the leaves,
Good for us to harvest and eat.

Yet today the enemy would say
Sugar only saves the day, candy canes laced with poison,
As he snickers up his sleeve
And panders a payday of death.

MASTER'S EYE

My God finger paints with stars,
Sparkling glitter scattered across a universal canvas
So vast the Milky Way is like a pinky print.

He can mold men from earth,
Colors flowers with His thoughts,
Forms storms in His frowns.

He sprinkles snow from storehouses brimming white.

My God loves me so much; He molded me,
Cradled me in my mother's womb.
What great wonder He has placed before me

As I swim in His sea and see
Fish brightly shimmering in coral trees,
Whales crying deep praise from ocean floor
to cresting shore.

Chiseled mountains scratch heaven from below;
Deep canyons flow, finger-drawn wanderings
To perfect ends.

God of wonder, shine forth in Your glory
Plainly seen by all with given eyes
And hearts humbled in spirited truth.

Perfect Tree

I see a tree twisted perfectly,
Formed for beams, with tortured seems
Splintered and hard, roughly carved
For pain.

I see God crying, perfect stain running
Down pierced feet to dry ground,
Steaming the stains of sin, mottling our skin,
Promising life.

For a dark death has come to one so innocent.
The heavens seek justice as my Lord says no
And enters a place reserved for sinners,
A place so ripe with wrong

That the earth rumbles in righteous anger
and hell still trembles,

For it is done.

TAPPING ON THE GLASS

My plane is late,
My flight soon to be cancelled.
The hard floor is a poor bed
Next to a socket, bringing life to my phone.

A lucky one am I
To be able to follow the storm up the coast,
Trapped here with most
Everyone else,

Lying under the glow of an aquarium
Home to a single fish, stunningly blue,
Circling endlessly in a clear prison,
Longing for the dark and quiet time,

Followed in every turn by the eyes of a young girl
Tapping gently on the prison walls,
Lost in the beauty of something she has never seen before,
An ocean creature caught far from the city.

As I sleep, I dream of tapping and Jesus,
He is standing at my window now,
Waving for me to come out to the better life beyond,
But I will circle one more lap,

Waiting for the dark and quiet time.

SHACKLES

What holds me so tightly to my comfort?
Is it the joy in these walls and the bills that built them?
Is it a need to be the same or fear of being different?
Is it a lack of truth or a blinding lie?
Is it a fear of failing,
A reminder of some falling,
Or a lazy pace brought on by abused grace?

A pampered child unwilling to share his toys
With brothers I refuse to see
And sisters I pretend cannot be.

LOSING MY FAITH

Accidents happen; it is easy to see.
Just look at the results called you and me.
Drunkards and druggies, liars and fools...
We are not exceptions when the enemy rules.

Still we cling to a faith that's been published and read,
Never a theory, the Darwinian thread,
To keep us all thinking life is just fate
Till we die and are met at the heavenly gate

By the one who loves us and made us His own
By choosing to die on a cross not His own.
For in love we are washed in the blood of my God,
Innocent blood spilt by nail, lash, and rod.

For I've never loved me as much as He does.
I find this flesh is still foul and wants what it was.
Despite this rejection, He stands at my door
And knocks oh so gently, still loving me more,

While I quietly seek truth through a veil of illusion,
Seeking to find some Christian solution,
When the answer is as plain as the nose on my face:
I am created by God and saved by His Grace.

Lovers Lie

Can a body be a god?
Is any curve perfect enough to defy
The reality
Of a God who loves you and I?

The whole of woman and the sign of man,
Created beings, dust and sand...
Can a body ever be a god?

Why chase it more than Him?
Why trust falsely in a whim?
For fantasy has an empty ring in real time,

And no man or woman worshiped can save.

Color Bar

Evergreen and hibiscus red,
Ocean blue on light sky blue
Bordering thunder gray, trailing to moonless black,

All to start again in sunrise orange and pure cloud white.
I wish I could paint half as well
With canary yellow and robin egg blue,
But as only a man created by You,

I must wonder at emerald green hummingbirds.

CREATED THINGS

I am hungry for hope,
For a man needs more than the wolf or bear.
They feed and breed, driven by need,
While man perishes in the lack of peace
Found in the absence of God.

Not absent by fact, not absent in truth,
But disguised in lies woven by neglect and knowledge.
For I have learned the myth of chance;
We have swallowed the lie of randomly formed life,
Leaving our greatest love on the shelf of myth.

WORTHY

Grace bound hand and foot,
Left outside in the rain like
Trash on pick-up day.

What can I say but why
Would You die for a bum like this
Unwashed fool in a city street?

Take a bath, stinky fool,
Drooling in a drunken stupor
Trying to forget...something horrid

Done in the grip of some false god.
Why bind to a cross created
By foolish choices made in rage

And fear?

For in the heart of God,
I am Worthy,
Even if in my heart,

He is not.

MOUNTAINS FALL

My heart is an icy mountain.
It formed with time,
Growing thick and tall in the winters of solitude,
Living the cold truth of the world's endless lies.

I am the fountain of my heart,
A heart forged by godless fires,
Swollen and putrid, marinated in lust and desires.
I speak of things that should not be,

For a devil plays my soul like it's his own
Or maybe soon to be.

Yet my mustard seed grows,
And my roots sink deep;
Into Godly soil they reach, in a desperate need,
To find a timeless love well hidden,

Until the day soon bidden
When prayer may cast my dead mountain
Into the Living Waters,
Drenched in the endless sea

Of forgiveness...

JUDGEMENT

I remember the walk of judgement,
Carrying the burden of bad choices
And the knowledge that they were unchanging,
Unyielding millstones warped tightly into my heart strings.
I remember the crushing fear of death and its promise
of nothing.
But one brave Man embraced the will of God
And accepted an impossible mission for one weak in
flesh like me.
Spirit filled and mercy bound, He walked an earthly path
And demanded our freedom, in a silent voice,
even when they laughed in the face of His needed death.
For the keys to nothing have been wrestled from a grip
Belonging to the father of lies, one condemned,
By the God who some say cannot be,
But He is truth and Savior to me.